The Judas Spirit
The Spirit of a Betrayer

by
Leon Shook

The Judas Spirit — The Spirit of a Betrayer
ISBN 0-927936-43-7
Copyright © 1993
Pastor Leon Shook
Power Source Ministries
4251 North Stratford Lane
Wichita, KS 67226

Published by Vincom, Inc.
P. O. Box 702400
Tulsa, OK 74170
(918) 254-1276

Dedication

I dedicate this book to my Lord and Savior, Jesus Christ; to my parents, Jesse and Dolly Shook; to Apostle Louis Greenup, Jr.; to my wife, Linda, and all my kids!

A special thank you to: Nina Shaw, Nancy Mehl, Jeanette Wilson, Larry Prothro, Danny Wingard and Lewis Burgar for their encouragement.

Leon Shook

Contents

Foreword

Never has there been a more timely book written to the Body of Christ than *The Judas Spirit* by Pastor Leon Shook. Through his writing, Pastor Shook sends a warning to every Christian leader and layman alike about the spirit of betrayal that has raised its ugly head in today's churches.

The Judas spirit is not a new thing. Actually, it originated in heaven in the presence of God in Lucifer himself. In the book of Isaiah, Lucifer, the picture of pride and rebellion, declared five times, "I will" as he proclaimed his rebellion. For this act of treason, he and one-third of the angels were kicked out of heaven. But Jesus, the picture of humility, always proclaimed, **Not My will, but Thy will be done**.

Just as Satan tries the same tricks on believers today that he has used for thousands of years, so this spirit has been used by him to sow seeds of rebellion for thousands of years. It began with the first brothers, Cain and Abel, when Cain killed his brother, Abel, out of jealousy and rebellion. Again, it appeared in the form of Dathan and Abiram when they rebelled against the authority of Moses and Aaron. Even Joseph's eleven brothers rose in jealousy and rebelled against him when he shared the dream God had given him about his family bowing in submission to him. It returned in the form of Absalom's rebellion when he attempted to steal the kingdom from his father, David. And in the greatest betrayal of all, Lucifer entered Judas, one of the twelve disciples, and put into his heart to betray the Son of God Himself (Luke 22:3; John 13:2).

God is a God of order, organization and authority. Everything in creation shows forth His divine order. So it is in the Body of Christ. God has given to the Church gifts to equip, build and instruct the saints of God. These gifts are apostles, prophets, evangelists, pastors and teachers (Ephesians 4:8-13). This is His divine order and authority in the Church. The Apostle Paul, in his writings to the church at Rome, said, **Let every soul be subject unto the higher powers. For there is no power but of God: the powers that be are ordained of God** (Romans 13:1). Rebellion is a work of the flesh (Galatians 5:19-21), and it reflects a mentality of immaturity. When there was division in the Corinthian church, with saints choosing their favorite leader (**One saith, I am of Paul; and another, I am of Apollos**), Paul said they were carnally minded. They were fleshly minded, or in other words, they were meatheads!

In almost every case of rebellion in a church, whether it is flock against the pastor, assistant pastor against the pastor, or deacons and elders against the pastor, there is an underlying reason for the treason. Though these reasons will be hidden in a cloak of so-called "spiritual" reasons, they are in fact plain old jealousy, envy and the desire for money, power and position.

Through this inspired book, Pastor Shook pulls the cloak off this rebellion, exposes it for what it is and warns the Church of the consequences of such a vile act of treason against the ordained authority of God. We must resist the devil and not give place to him and allow him to cause this division in the Church.

I highly recommend that every Christian read this book and be forewarned of the consequences of rebellion in the Church of Jesus Christ.

Apostle Louis Greenup, Jr.

Introduction

In the world and in the Church today, there are many spirits at work — One is holy and the others are evil. Isn't it interesting that one Holy Spirit is enough to control and defeat all of the other spirits?

Demonic spirits are identified by their assigned tasks. For example, pornography is controlled by the spirits of sexual perversion, greed, immorality and hate. There are also spirits of strife, division and envy. Every sinful act of man has an ungodly spirit behind it. The prince or high commander is Satan himself.

The leaders or directors of these demon spirits are classed according to their rank and job description. They are somewhat organized, though they often operate in confusion, for their leader is the author of confusion. Even at their best (or should I say, their worst?), they are in no way as organized as the godly rank and file of angelic spirits.

We will address one of the confused ranks of cowardly spirits in this book, called the *Judas spirit*, also known as *the spirit of the betrayer*.

As you probably remember, Judas betrayed Jesus Christ. His complete title was Judas Iscariot, not to be confused with Judas, the brother of James. As you might remember, Judas Iscariot was the treasurer (Administrator of Finances) for the ministry of Jesus.

Unfortunately, the Judas spirit is still operating in the Church. We will see by looking at scripture that the Judas spirit, if allowed to do so, can cause people to betray even those who are very close to them. It is time to expose him and rid the Church of his devastating influence.

You, dear children, are from God and have overcome them, because the one who is in you is greater than the one who is in the world.

1 John 4:4

Greater is the One Who has been revealed in you than any demon who has been exposed in this world (Shook's paraphrase!).

An exposed demon is a defeated demon!

1

The Nature and Character of the Judas Spirit

He called his twelve disciples to him and gave them authority to drive out evil spirits and to heal every disease and sickness.

These are the names of the twelve apostles: first, Simon (who is called Peter) and his brother Andrew; James son of Zebedee, and his brother John;

Philip and Bartholomew; Thomas and Matthew the tax collector; James son of Alphaeus, and Thaddaeus;

Simon the Zealot and Judas Iscariot, who betrayed him.

These twelve Jesus sent out with the following instructions: "Do not go among the Gentiles or enter any town of the Samaritans.

"Go rather to the lost sheep of Israel.

"As you go, preach this message: `The kingdom of heaven is near.'

"Heal the sick, raise the dead, cleanse those who have leprosy, drive out demons. Freely you have received, freely give."

Matthew 10:1-8

From this scripture, it appears that Judas Iscariot was fully accepted and involved in the work of Jesus' ministry. Verse 1 does *not* say that everyone *except Judas* was given authority and sent to preach the message, raise the dead, drive out demons and heal disease and sickness.

Scripture says Jesus called the twelve disciples, gave them authority and sent them out. It would appear from this scripture that a person with a Judas spirit can do mighty things for God.

It is obvious that Judas, a man of fiery passion and greed, did not understand or comprehend that Jesus was truly the Messiah. The Sonship of Jesus was vague to him.

Judas Exalts Himself

Judas was said to be a Jewish Nationalist. History portrays him as a violent, outspoken man, one who wanted to be free from Roman rule. He was looking for a warlike Messiah Who would come and destroy his enemies.

It appears that Judas did not really know how to receive this servant of man named Jesus. Judas' main problem, however, wasn't misunderstanding Jesus. His primary problems were jealousy, envy, greed and pride. The very things that caused Satan to be thrown out of heaven made Judas a prime target to be controlled by a Judas spirit.

> How you have fallen from heaven, O morning star, son of the dawn! You have been cast down to the earth, you who once laid low the nations!
>
> You said in your heart, "I will ascend to heaven; I will raise my throne above the stars of God; I will sit enthroned on the mount of assembly, on the utmost heights of the sacred mountain.
>
> "I will ascend above the tops of the clouds; I will make myself like the Most High."
>
> But you are brought down to the grave, to the depths of the pit.
>
> Isaiah 14:12-15

Judas has even been accused of stealing from Jesus' ministry funds.

Some Church People Are Still Stealing From God

As awful as that sounds, thousands of people in churches today aren't tithing. They are doing the same thing Judas did. Tithing is a commandment, so to not tithe is robbing from God.

"I the Lord do not change. So you, O descendants of Jacob, are not destroyed.

"Ever since the time of your forefathers you have turned away from my decrees and have not kept them. Return to me, and I will return to you," says the Lord Almighty. "But you ask, `How are we to return?'

"Will a man rob God? Yet you rob me. But you ask, `How do we rob you?' In tithes and offerings.

"You are under a curse — the whole nation of you — because you are robbing me.

"Bring the whole tithe into the storehouse, that there may be food in my house. Test me in this," says the Lord Almighty, "and see if I will not throw open the floodgates of heaven and pour out so much blessing that you will not have room enough for it.

"I will prevent pests from devouring your crops, and the vines in your fields will not cast their fruit," says the Lord Almighty.

"Then all nations will call you blessed, for yours will be a delightful land," says the Lord Almighty.

"You have said harsh things against me," says the Lord. "Yet you ask, `What have we said against you?'

"You have said, `It is futile to serve God. What did we gain by carrying out his requirements and going about like mourners before the Lord Almighty?

"`But now we call the arrogant blessed. Certainly the evildoers prosper, and even those who challenge God escape.'"

Then those who feared the Lord talked with each other, and the Lord listened and heard. A scroll of remembrance was written in his presence concerning those who feared the Lord and honored his name.

"They will be mine," says the Lord Almighty, "in the day when I make up my treasured possession. I will spare them, just as in compassion a man spares his son who serves him."

Malachi 3:6-17

One can only wonder how Judas lived with Jesus so closely, saw His miracles, yet didn't know Jesus as the Son of God. Even to the end of Jesus' life, with all the supernatural power He displayed, Judas seemed unaware of Jesus' identity. It was the spirit behind Judas' actions that blinded him to God's divine purposes.

Judas Spirit Manifests When Woman Anoints Jesus For Burial

In Matthew 26:6-12, we find the Judas spirit in action when a blessing was bestowed upon Jesus. The reaction of the twelve disciples was the exact opposite of what you would expect.

While Jesus was in Bethany in the home of a man known as Simon the Leper,

A woman came to him with an alabaster jar of very expensive perfume, which she poured on his head as he was reclining at the table.

When the disciples saw this, they were indignant. "Why this waste?" they asked.

"This perfume could have been sold at a high price and the money given to the poor."

Aware of this, Jesus said to them, "Why are you bothering this woman? She has done a beautiful thing to me.

"The poor you will always have with you, but you will not always have me.

"When she poured this perfume on my body, she did it to prepare me for burial."

These verses describe the nature and character of the Judas spirit, which is still actively at work today. How many church boards or church members would be indignant if their pastor was honored in some way? How many might feel it would be a waste to give him something valuable?

When the woman poured the expensive perfume over the head of the Lord, all of the disciples were indignant — not just Judas. **Why this waste?** they asked. Since all of the disciples were apparently indignant, it would seem that anyone who allows himself to be used by this spirit will be.

Notice, however, that all but Judas were satisfied that the pouring of the oil was a good thing after Jesus explained its purpose. **She has done a beautiful thing to me...When she poured this perfume on my body, she did it to prepare my body for burial.**

Motives of The Judas Spirit: Divide and Destroy

Judas immediately went to the chief priests and plotted to betray Jesus for thirty pieces of silver.

As a lay person, you might think of a betrayer as someone close to you who lets you down or purposely sets you up for a fall. Although it is true that the spirits of strife, division, greed and jealousy are behind these kinds of betrayals, the Judas spirit is of a different class. It is a combination of all of these spirits and more.

This offense is made from one sheep to another, but the Judas spirit works sheep against shepherd, associate shepherd against senior shepherd, shepherd against shepherd, minister against minister and ministries against ministries. All church workers and leaders — elders, deacons, pastors, ministers and ministries — must guard against being used or influenced by the Judas spirit.

The motive of the Judas spirit isn't just to cause division between two Christians. Its motive is to destroy entire churches, cities and countries.

The Judas spirit is never satisfied or settled as long as there is one God-fearing, Bible-believing person to oppose him. He will continue his work to divide and conquer. The unfortunate truth is that church traditions and governmental procedures have aided him in his ungodly pursuits and maneuvers.

Elder and deacon boards that are headed up by immature Christians or people who don't even confess to be born again, have opened churches up to the Judas spirit and made it easy for this spirit to operate.

To expect an unsaved person to make mature spiritual decisions on behalf of a church is beyond my understanding. Unfortunately, there are churches who are doing just that. They are depending on these unsaved people, placed in positions of authority, who have no knowledge of the things of God, to give godly direction. No wonder some pastors move from church to church and never see any fruit from their ministries.

How can two walk together unless they agree? (Shook's paraphrase of Amos 3:3.) Agree on what? The first area of agreement should be that a man must be born again. If we have no agreement on this guideline, then there will be no agreement at all.

2
The Chief Shepherd Versus the Judas Spirit

In this chapter, we will deal with the potential for the betrayal of the shepherd by his own sheep. Observations made in this chapter and subsequent chapters are dependent upon a pastor being called of God to his position. Most pastors are, although some are not.

Scripture calls the person who acts as a shepherd, but who isn't called or anointed for that position of God, a hireling.

> **"I am the good shepherd. The good shepherd lays down his life for the sheep.**
>
> **"The hired hand [hireling] is not the shepherd who owns the sheep. So when he sees the wolf coming, he abandons the sheep and runs away. Then the wolf attacks and scatters it.**
>
> **"The man runs away because he is a hired hand and cares nothing for the sheep."**
>
> **John 10:11-13**

It is not our responsibility to judge which pastors are called of God and which are not. Only God has the wisdom to judge and determine that. God is omnipotent. He sees the thoughts and motives of a person's heart. Our response should be to pray and let God do the placing and replacing.

According to this scripture in John, if trouble does come to a church and they have a hired hand [a hireling] instead of a pastor, the flock will scatter. God is saying that a hireling will not be able to keep a church together when trouble comes. Knowing the condition of the world today, trouble will come, and when it does, the true nature and character of a pastor will be revealed.

Some pastors are hirelings, but most are called men and women of God who truly desire to see God's Kingdom established on this earth. Do not be naive enough to think, however, that every person who fills the pulpit as a pastor is truly called of God. We should have peace in knowing that we can trust God to judge and decide who will represent Him.

A hireling who poses as a pastor will have a short, unpleasant tenure. He may be an efficient political and social figure, but he cannot stand as a spokesman for God on the sole basis of talent and personality. It takes the anointing of God and depth of character to be a spiritual leader. In churches where talent and personality are favored over the anointing, hirelings will be found!

Basically, it boils down to the fact that a church will have the type of leader they are willing to tolerate. It is up to the Body to pray and put a demand on the anointing and the gifts that are resident in a pastor. If they do not, anyone with talent and personality can serve them and their social agenda.

In this chapter, we will deal with sheep who spiritually and physically come against and defy the call of one who is anointed of God.

Sheep Against Shepherd

The shepherd of a church who has sheep motivated by a Judas spirit will find that he (or she) is facing a group of people who normally want to keep him (or her) poor and humble. They are offended if the pastor is blessed in any way above what they feel he should be. If the pastor gets a new car, they would wonder what was wrong with the old one, regardless of its condition.

Any expenditure for personal or even for church would be challenged as wasteful unless the sheep had need of the item themselves. Just like Judas Iscariot, if they become indignant, they will betray the shepherd by seeking others to agree with them. They might even seek to have him removed as pastor.

It's hard to believe that something as dumb as a sheep would try to control the very one who protects and feeds him. I'm not trying to offend anyone, but sheep aren't really that intelligent, and left to themselves, they will usually starve to death or be eaten by some wild animal. A pastor provides protective spiritual covering for the sheep. Their life, health and prosperity are covered under his anointing.

With that in mind, isn't it amazing that a sheep would think he (or she) is more capable of leading a flock than the shepherd?

As a child, I attended a small church that was my home church from the time I was seven until I left for Bible college at eighteen. Everything I knew spiritually I learned there. We hadn't seen a new person or family come and stay for many years.

After my sisters grew up and left that church, I was the only teenager left. Being the only young person didn't make for a very vibrant youth group! It was also obvious that the prospects for church growth weren't too great!

People were satisfied to occupy the same pew every Sunday, talk about how evil the world was and how everything was going to the devil. They weren't willing to do anything about it, however, like witness to neighbors or invite friends to church. (It's probably a good thing they didn't, because if their friends and neighbors were hungry for the Word or for Christian love, they would have starved to death!)

The couple who started the work had been there for many years. They were a loving couple who had grown up in the area and, after becoming Christians, they felt that God had called them to pastor in the town in which they had been raised. It was under their ministry that I was saved, for which I will be eternally grateful.

The pastor was a dedicated, hard-working man with a strong anointing to teach and pastor. He was never allowed to reach his full potential, however, because he had to hold down a full-time job besides the duties of a pastor to make ends meet. Eventually, he became so overworked and worn out that he left. I believe his weariness wasn't so much because of his other job as it was a lack of support and love from the majority of the church Body. He wasn't required to work outside the church because we were a poor church. He did so because our church's man-made doctrines taught that we were to keep our pastors poor so they would be humble. How ridiculous that seems now!

After he left, God sent a couple to pastor who were excited about winning the city to Jesus Christ. They were unaware of the nature and character of the leadership of the church. Suddenly, new people arrived and new converts came looking for a place to do something to help the Body. The town wondered about the growth and excitement of the church, where before, they had wondered about that strange little church on the corner! They opened up and received us and the new pastors as a positive addition to the city.

As God did mighty things in the eyes of the townspeople, a small group of people, whom I believe were motivated by a Judas spirit, plotted on how to get rid of this troublesome couple —the pastor and his wife. "How dare they come and disturb this comfortable little church," they must have thought. One man was foolish enough to stand up and give a satirical testimony as to how he felt our church was really special in that we actually allowed ex-sinners to attend.

While under heavy spiritual and verbal attack, the pastor couple continued to try to bring love and unity into the Body. The elders and the small group of troublemakers began to withhold their tithes, and they spread terrible lies and rumors throughout the town.

Slowly, they undermined the pastors until most of the young converts became confused and discouraged and left. I can't describe to you the sadness and agony I felt as a young man, watching people I admired and trusted turn so ugly and hateful.

Eventually, they did get a vote of the leadership and decided that the pastors must leave. God never intended for any man to decide when His servants are to stay or go. He alone has the authority to do that.

It was only after death threats were made and the police called for the protection of the pastor and his family that they decided to leave. What a hideous testimony to any city on how Christian brothers and sisters are to act!

The saddest part of the story is that even after the pastors left, the hatred and bitterness lingered. Less than a year after this took place, all three of the elders and some of the small group of betrayers became ill and died.

It isn't healthy to be a betrayer in the Body of Christ.

3

Church Leaders and the Judas Spirit

Elders and Deacons

Elders and deacons are to serve the pastors by serving the people. They are called to do the things that the pastor does not have the time to do. Pastors should not be expected to do all of the hospital visitations, head up every church workday and do all the counseling and teaching.

The office of an elder or a deacon comes with work attached to it. Their ministry is to free the pastor of some of his duties to allow him time for prayer and study of the Word. Spiritually, one of their primary duties is that of an intercessor. They are to shield the pastor from attack and from any evil report. They are to pray and hold his arms up when he becomes weary.

I would simply ask you again, "How in the world can an immature Christian or an unsaved person ever fulfill this calling?"

Church leaders, elders and deacons can move off course from their scriptural calling as servants of the people and armor-bearers to the pastor to become the financial watchdogs of the church if they submit to this controlling spirit. This usually means they kick about how every penny is spent and where it is being spent. God never intended for church elders to control the church's purse strings!

Any elder who moves from the ministry level to the watchdog level will be miserable and will also succeed in making the pastor miserable.

It is a personal observation that in several churches, the first people considered as elders are the ones who are the most successful in finances and business. Financial wisdom is a great asset if you are looking for a business partner, and it won't hinder a person from being qualified to be an elder, but it is a poor substitute for the scriptural qualifications required to fill this position.

> Here is a trustworthy saying: If anyone sets his heart on being an overseer [bishop or elder], he desires a noble task.
>
> Now the overseer must be above reproach, the husband of but one wife, temperate, self-controlled, respectable, hospitable, able to teach,
>
> Not given to drunkenness, not violent but gentle, not quarrelsome, not a lover of money.
>
> He must manage his own family well and see that his children obey him with proper respect.
>
> (If anyone does not know how to manage his own family, how can he take care of God's church?)
>
> He must not be a recent convert, or he may become conceited and fall under the same judgment as the devil.
>
> He must also have a good reputation with outsiders, so that he will not fall into disgrace and into the devil's trap.
>
> Deacons, likewise, are to be men worthy of respect, sincere, not indulging in much wine, and not pursuing dishonest gain.
>
> They must keep hold of the deep truths of the faith with a clear conscience.
>
> They must first be tested; and then if there is nothing against them, let them serve as deacons.
>
> In the same way, their wives are to be women worthy of respect, not malicious talkers but temperate and trustworthy in everything.

> A deacon must be the husband of one wife and must manage his children and his household well.
>
> 1 Timothy 3:1-12

According to this scripture, the office of a deacon requires almost the same qualifications as an elder. These offices are only to be filled by persons who have good fruit coming forth in their lives and in the lives of their family members.

It seems bizarre to me that a pastor would ever be required to justify anything God told him to do to a board of elders or deacons. Granted, we all are to be accountable, but to whom? God is well able to communicate His desires. He is well able to place or replace whom He chooses, and if a pastor refuses to follow His leading, that is exactly what God will do.

Elders and deacons should be sought out for counsel, but they should not make the final decisions, nor should they have the right to be offended if the pastor feels God's leading in a different direction. How many pastors have dreaded the next board meeting, knowing they will have to fight for every item needed to perform the ministry to which God has called them?

How we ever came to the conclusion that God called our churches to be democracies I'll never know! If you will notice in events throughout the Bible, the majority vote was usually wrong! There was never a majority vote of the children of Israel when deciding to leave Egypt. Instead, the procedure was that Moses heard from God, and after hearing, he told the people what God said. Then, the children of Israel obeyed. Had the exodus from Egypt been left to a vote, the Jewish people would most likely be speaking Egyptian even today! Also remember that it was a majority vote that kept *THE MAJORITY* of the children of

Israel from entering the promised land. (See Numbers 13 and 14.)

The Associate Pastor

The ministry that a chief shepherd entrusts to his associate is a very sacred thing. An associate's foremost responsibility is to see that the vision God has given the chief shepherd is brought to completion. If the associate entertains negative thoughts or is offended when the pastor's vision interferes or hinders his vision and ministry desires, then the associate risks being used by the Judas spirit.

Satan enjoys tearing apart a ministry team that God has supernaturally put together. What sometimes happens in these situations when an associate is offended and betrays the pastor's trust is that the pastor's ministry is hindered. But what about the associate pastor's vision? What usually happens to the associate is that his vision never comes to reality. However, *if the associate sees that the pastor's vision is fulfilled, God will see to it that his vision will also be fulfilled.*

Church Workers and Leaders

Church workers and leaders must guard their hearts. The best way to guard your heart is to guard *who* and *what* you listen to. The Judas spirit loves to talk and looks for an open ear to hear him.

The people who work in a church or the leaders controlled by a Judas spirit usually are complainers. *They are openly submissive but inwardly rebellious!* They look for shortcomings in the pastor and love to gossip with others about them. Secretly, they hope to see the pastor fail. Sometimes they are difficult for a pastor to spot because of their submissive mask.

Unless the Holy Spirit is asked to reveal them, they often go unnoticed by the pastor. That is, until they make their motives known. Any pastor who has any doubt about the motives or the spirit of a leader or worker should ask the Holy Spirit for the hidden things to be revealed.

...He [God] will bring to light what is hidden in darkness and will expose the motive of men's hearts....
1 Corinthians 4:5

The pastor should discreetly seek the opinions of the person's co-workers and fellow ministers. Normally, if you ask enough people, you will get an honest evaluation of the person's true spirit and character.

Are they complainers? Are they openly submissive to your face but rebellious toward you around others? Are they slow to admit their own mistakes but quick to point out the mistakes of others? Do they suffer from a low self-esteem but are quick to boast of their own abilities, lacking scriptural humility? Do they seem upset when you or others are promoted or blessed above them?

Even though the evaluations of co-workers and fellow ministers should be sought only after seeking God's direction, a leader should have a strong enough relationship with his staff that they will feel comfortable to bring the concern of a co-worker's motives to him. The pastor must then depend upon the Holy Spirit to discern if those concerns are real or not.

4

Administrators and the Judas Spirit

Then one of the Twelve — the one called Judas Iscariot — went to the chief priests

And asked, "What are you willing to give me if I hand him over to you?" So they counted out for him thirty silver coins.

From then on Judas watched for an opportunity to hand him over.

Matthew 26:14-16

Generally, church treasurers and administrators tend to be the most affected and attacked by the Judas spirit. They should be the most trustworthy, tight-lipped people on any church staff. Like Judas, they are in charge of seeing that the needs and bills of the ministry are met each month.

They can become offended if a pastor seeks to expand an already financially demanding ministry. They must guard their hearts and mouths to keep anyone from knowing that an already taxed budget is about to become more so.

A minister of finance and administration should never lose sight of the fact that it is the pastor who hears the voice of God and receives instruction as to the church's growth and direction. If they fail to acknowledge this, they will put themselves in a position that they are neither called nor anointed to fill. (In short, they are not the pastor!)

A primary danger is that the Administrators of Finance not allow money to become their focus of ministry. If administrators minister *to* finances instead of administrating the finances, there is the danger of money becoming their object of ministry or service.

By definition, ministry means "to serve." Money should not be served. Whatever or whomever you love, you will serve. The *love of money* is the root of all evil (1 Timothy 6:10). Remember, Judas betrayed Jesus after being paid only thirty silver coins —a very small sum to condemn the Son of the Living God to His death!

Money cannot be ministered to; only *people* can receive ministry. Church administrators are first and foremost ministers or servants unto the pastor, then to the Body. They are secondly the administrators of finances, and finances are needed to minister to people.

It is the administrator's responsibility to see that the finances are in good order for the pastor and the Body. It is not his responsibility to determine *how* the money is to be used to minister.

Another area that can lead to temptation is knowing the pastor's salary. If his salary is large, it can lead to jealousy and envy. If and when a pastor is blessed beyond his normal salary with a love gift or an offering, those who handle church finances can become indignant. "What a waste! He gets paid plenty well. Why should he get blessed like that?" Why indeed!

Remember when the woman poured the expensive perfume over Jesus' head? (Matthew 26:7). "Yes," you might say, "but that was in preparation for Jesus' death and burial." That's true. Jesus would, in a very short time, lay His life down for you and me, His sheep. Isn't that, in fact, what your pastor does every day — lay his life and desires down for you, his sheep?

Whatever is sown will also be reaped. **Do not be deceived: God cannot be mocked. A man reaps what he sows** (Galatians 6:7). God desires to bless you just as much as He desires to bless your pastor. **God does not show favoritism** (Acts 10:34).

Having been on staff of the same church for several years, I have watched our church grow in numbers and the facilities quadruple in size. We have gone from a Body who had no permanent home to one who has outgrown one facility and is well on its way to outgrowing another!

During all of the growth, we felt God's leading to purchase and operate several local Christian radio stations. I dare say that if these things would have been dependent upon a vote of most church boards or congregations, it would never have been accomplished.

However, I can honestly say that with the church Body we now have, most likely we would have received a *positive vote* had it been done that way. How do I know that? Because the people have been so faithful with their time and finances to support this work.

It was strenuous to the financial staff to stay in faith month by month as the church budget increased, but for the most part they did stay in faith and in one accord without complaint and without worry.

5

The Judas Spirit Can Control Even the Very Elect

Pastors, Ministers and Ministries

Then the mother of Zebedee's sons came to Jesus with her sons and, kneeling down, asked a favor of him.

"What is it you want?" he asked. She said, "Grant that one of these two sons of mine may sit at your right and the other at your left in your kingdom."

"You don't know what you are asking," Jesus said to them. "Can you drink the cup that I am going to drink?" "We can," they answered.

Jesus said to them, "You will indeed drink from my cup, but to sit at my right or left is not for me to grant. These places belong to those for whom they have been prepared by my Father."

When the ten heard about this, they were indignant with the two brothers.

Jesus called them together and said, "You know that the rulers of the Gentiles lord it over them, and their high officials exercise authority over them.

"Not so with you. Instead, whoever wants to become great among you must be your servant,

"And whoever wants to be first must be your slave —

"Just as the Son of Man did not come to be served, but to serve, and to give his life as a ransom for many."

Matthew 20:20-28

We must choose to serve. Paul referred to himself on several occasions as a slave or a servant of Christ. Jesus made you a son or daughter of God through salvation but you must then choose to be a servant. Servanthood is a matter of choice.

While looking for promotion, pastors can get into a competitive mindset. No man is your promoter, but it is the Lord who promotes based on what is in your heart.

There is a story told of a young man who had just come on staff of a church. His zeal for success caused him to work long, hard hours beyond what the job required. As he worked, he noticed an older man who had been on staff of the same church for several years. He noticed that the older man seemed to get very little done and had walked by his office on several occasions to find him asleep.

Finally, he could not tolerate the unfairness of the situation any longer, so he decided to go see the senior pastor about it. The pastor listened to all the young man had to say, then leaned back in his chair, and after a short pause for reflection, simply said, "Remember, it is God who keeps the books."

As the young man left the pastor's office, he walked by the co-worker's office and again, his co-worker was sitting behind his desk, his head down, sound asleep.

God does keep the books, and promotion comes from Him. **But it is God who judges: he brings one down, he exalts another** (Psalm 75:7).

A competitive spirit has no place in a church or ministry. One church leader in a large denominational church told me that his denomination sent out a publication on a regular basis that contained all the latest statistics on whose church had the most members. Whenever this newsletter came out, everyone stopped what they were doing and called each other to talk about who was on top for the month.

Jealousy and strife that often come from this type of competition can be tremendous, not to mention the discouragement one church might feel if they never made the list.

I personally refrain from participating in church sports groups because of the overwhelming competitiveness that is involved. I never grew accustomed to Christian brothers and sisters yelling and fighting over who did or did not make a point or goal. Personally, I am competitive, but mostly with myself. I push myself to always do better. In that sense, I suppose you could say I compete with myself.

I believe some of the competitiveness, jealousy and discouragement that is prevalent in our churches today is because God's people are not trusting in the Lord for promotion. A lack of scriptural humility has also opened the door for some pastors, ministers and ministries to be influenced and controlled by the Judas spirit.

I also believe that the Judas spirit is responsible for some of the blatant church-bashing events that have taken place over the last few years. The Judas spirit desires to destroy ministries. Don't be guilty of helping the devil!

This subject is too big to be covered completely in this book. However, I believe one event that could be used as an example of the spirit of betrayal would be the P.T.L. scandal —and that's just what it was — a scandal!

I was never an avid watcher of P.T.L., but I saw the program occasionally. I know several people, some inside the charismatic movement and some outside, who were dependent on P.T.L. for their spiritual growth and advancement. These people were devastated when it crumbled.

Many of my non-charismatic co-ministers were openly disappointed when the P.T.L. events were revealed. Although some people seemed to relish the fall of such a large charismatic influence, most people were profoundly disappointed. Many people hoped and prayed that this ministry was for real. I believe it was of God. But not only did the charismatics suffer because of this ministry's transgressions, the entire Church suffered because of its fall. The good news is that many ministries have continued to grow in the face of P.T.L.'s devastation.

God took what the devil meant for evil and turned it around for good. Because of P.T.L.'s fall, there is a new sense of integrity and accountability in many churches. In that sense, the P.T.L. events served as a blessing in disguise.

However, what about all the people and ministries who lost faith as a result of this devastation? Some people lost all hope and turned away from the rest of God's family because of this man's fall. That is the danger of following after a man of God and not God in the man. We must trust in the One Who never fails — Jesus Christ!

I believe the P.T.L. scandal occurred because of a combination of jealousy, greed and a betrayal spirit. Whenever you have success and notoriety, someone will look for a way to knock you down a notch!

P.T.L. was a great threat to Satan's kingdom so he gave it great attention. If you are a threat, the devil will know your name, your address, the names of your family members, the church you attend, the car you drive and where you bank. You will have his attention. He can't touch you, however, if you don't give him an opening. That doesn't mean he won't try. It just means **no weapon formed against you will prosper** if you don't lower your spiritual guard through sin.

There was an opening given in the P.T.L. affair through a combination of sinful acts, and I believe one person, a fellow minister who was jealous and offended, started the steamroller on a roll! He devised a plan to catch this anointed, but weak man, in a trap that he devised and planned while under the influence of a Judas spirit, which, I believe, set the stage for the betrayal of the P.T.L. leadership.

He found a harlot (I'm curious how he knew where to find one) who agreed to prostitute herself for a fee. He promised her that no one would know but him and her. She would receive a lot of money and this anointed but weak man would get what he truly deserved — to be shamed and lose the ministry God had given him.

In the end, however, the Church and the world did know, and she never received a lot of money as she had been promised. That is why, I believe, her attacks were so vicious against the fallen leadership of P.T.L.

Did this man deserve what happened to him? I don't know. Did he do everything that the press, television and the courts accused him of? I don't know. I tend to believe very little of what the news media says. It has been proven over and over again that they print and report the news as they desire it to be, not necessarily as it is.

The more important question I'd like to ask is this: Did God get any glory from what took place? Did His Church look better for what happened? Definitely not! We, the Church, were betrayed.

Unfortunately, the potential for this type of situation to happen again is still present. As long as weak men are in control, and competition, jealousy and greed are allowed to thrive in men's hearts, there will be fertile ground for the Judas spirit to take root.

One need only watch the harlot's true nature be revealed to know that her innocence was just an act. Meanwhile, the Church suffers ridicule, and an admittedly guilty but forgiven man of God, sits in a cell, a victim of his own actions and the influence of the Judas spirit.

6

How Close Can a Judas Spirit-Controlled Person Get to You?

How close was Judas to Jesus and the other disciples? Just as close as any disciple was to another! Jesus knew from the beginning that Judas would betray Him, just as He knew that Peter would deny Him and the other disciples would desert Him in His darkest hour.

Judas was treated no differently by Jesus than were the other disciples. We know this, because when Jesus said at the Last Supper, **one of you will betray me**, not one of them had a clue as to who it was.

Jesus was troubled in Spirit and testified:

> **"I tell you the truth, one of you is going to betray me."**
> **His disciples stared at one another, at a loss to know which of them he meant.**
>
> **John 13:21,22**

In fact, each felt it could have been himself personally. Jesus allowed Judas to be a part of His ministry because He knew that prophecy must be fulfilled.

> **Even my close friend, whom I trusted, he who shared my bread, has lifted up his heel against me.**
>
> **Psalm 41:9**

As a pastor, you have no such Bible prophecy that must come into reality in this hour. If you have anyone —

even someone close to you — who has a Judas spirit, deal with that person. If he (or she) will not change, then have the courage to remove them. For the sake of the other sheep and ministers in your church, you can't allow such a person to stay. A pastor who allows this kind of spirit to remain and propagate itself will appear weak and out of control of the ministry God has entrusted to him.

So how does one rid himself of a Judas spirit in his midst without removing the person? Sometimes you can't, because some people enjoy having this spirit around them. To know how to remove this spirit from your church, you must first be able to identify him.

We will reveal him in a later chapter, but first we will answer the question, "How does a person get himself in a place to be controlled by this spirit?"

7

Giving Place to the Judas Spirit

Dear friends, now we are children of God, and what we will be has not yet been made known. But we know when he [Jesus] appears, we shall be like him, for we shall see him as he is.

Everyone who has this hope in him purifies himself, just as he is pure.

Everyone who sins breaks the law; in fact, sin is lawlessness.

1 John 3:2-4

I would encourage you to read the entire book of 1 John, giving special attention to chapters 3 and 4.

How does one give place to the Judas spirit? Through sin. Jesus was sinless and never broke God's law. Because of that, the devil could never touch Him until Jesus allowed it. Jesus said, **No one takes it [my life] from me, but I lay it down of my own accord** (John 10:18). We, however, are not sinless. Romans 3:23 says, **For all have sinned and fall short of the glory of God.**

If we give place to the devil through unforgiven sins, allowing ourselves to be controlled by the Judas spirit, or we give a devil-controlled person a place to harass us through our own unforgiven sins, the devil will succeed in his attack against us. If we sin, we need to repent, which means to turn from sin. Jesus said, **If we confess our sins,**

he [God] **is faithful and just and will forgive us of our sins and purify us from all unrighteousness** (1 John 1:9).

Scripture says that **everything that does not come from faith is sin** (Romans 14:23). I dare say all of us have been out of faith at one time or another. We allow the Judas spirit to operate when we have an open door to sin. Needless to say, none of the events at P.T.L. would have happened if sin had not been allowed to overtake their leaders.

First John 3:11-24 talks about our need to love God and to love one another. First John 4:7,8 says:

> Dear friends, let us love one another, for love comes from God. Everyone who loves has been born of God and knows God.
>
> Whoever does not love does not know God, because God is love.

First John 5:2 says, **This is how we know that we love the children of God: by loving God and carrying out His commands**.... Verse 4 says, **For everyone born of God overcomes the world**....

To sin is just plain dumb! If you sow seeds of lawlessness, you will reap a harvest of like kind. If you are involved in sin, you put yourself under the law. If you put yourself under the law, you also place yourself under the judgment of the law.

No one but Jesus has ever been able to live sinless under the law. That is why God gives us grace. We physically walk out from under His protective grace when we sin. God's grace always covers and protects us spiritually and our soul and spirit are secure in Him, but when we sin, we place our physical being in a worldly arena, and we will be judged by the world. We are to be in the world but not of it. In other words, we should not place ourselves in a position where the world can sit in judgment of us.

We are to be judged only by God, through His grace, and His grace always judges us "not guilty" through the blood of Jesus Christ. Sin gives a physical place to the Judas spirit, and Satan will take full advantage of you when he has an open door.

> "Everything is permissible for me" — but not everything is beneficial. "Everything is permissible for me" — but I will not be mastered by anything.
>
> 1 Corinthians 6:12

> "Everything is permissible" — but not everything is beneficial. "Everything is permissible" — but not everything is constructive.
>
> Nobody should seek his own good, but the good of others.
>
> 1 Corinthians 10:23,24

Under God's grace, Paul says everything is lawful or permissible for him, but not everything is beneficial. Paul was not going to be mastered or controlled by anything. Whatever sin we willingly become a participant in will eventually be our master. It will master or control us unless we control it. Sin should not have any control over us, but we should be its master.

First Corinthians 10:24 says, **Nobody should seek his own good, but the good of others.** Love God with all you have and all you are, and love your neighbor as yourself.

When you sin, you sow seeds that will produce a harvest. That harvest will not only hurt you but it, most likely, will injure several others, sometimes multitudes.

While you are trying to pray a crop failure on your last crop of sin, you may miss that one person whose salvation could change the entire city in which you live. Changing cities for Christ will change countries, and changed countries will change the world. Think about it!

One verse in a child's song entitled, "Sin Busters," says, "If you're gonna sin, you ain't gonna win." That's just how it is!

8

Who Is the Judas Spirit?

Now the Feast of Unleavened Bread, called the Passover, was approaching,

And the chief priests and the teachers of the law were looking for some way to get rid of Jesus, for they were afraid of the people.

Then Satan entered Judas, called Iscariot, one of the Twelve.

And Judas went to the chief priests and the officers of the temple guard and discussed with them how he might betray Jesus.

They were delighted and agreed to give him money.

He consented, and watched for an opportunity to hand Jesus over to them when no crowd was present.

Luke 22:1-6

When Jesus began His earthly ministry, I believe a panic rumbled through the demonic camp. Never in all history had a man wreaked such havoc with Satan's plans of evil. No one ever destroyed the works of Satan as Jesus did. He defied every natural law, yet never broke any of God's laws. He was sinless and perfect in every way. I believe Satan knew that if he didn't stop Jesus, his reign of terror was finished. From the time God prophesied in Genesis 3:15, Satan watched for this man, Jesus, who would come from a virgin and oppose him and his kingdom.

Genesis 3:15 says:

> "And I will put enmity between you [Satan] and the
> woman, and between your offspring and hers; he [Jesus]
> will crush your head, and you will strike his heel."

What terrorized Satan even more was that now it
wasn't just Jesus who would cause him grief, but there
were twelve other men doing the works of Jesus. Satan
knew he had to do something quick.

Satan always looks for the weakest link. He looks for
the one most easily offended. When he finds him (or her),
he begins to work on their feelings of low self-worth and
lack of self-esteem. He needs someone made of flesh and
blood to allow him a body through whom he can legally
oppose Jesus. Satan is an illegal alien to this earth. Jesus
said that man must first be born of the water (the womb)
and then be born again of the Spirit (John 3:3-8).

Satan came into this world illegally. He was cast down
like a lightning bolt from heaven after he rebelled against
God (Luke 10:18). He was not born of a woman, so it was
illegal for him to have any authority on this earth unless
man gave him the authority through sin.

Luke 22:3,4 says:

> Then Satan entered Judas, called Iscariot, one of the
> Twelve.
> And Judas went to the chief priests and the officers of
> the temple guard and discussed with them how he might
> be able to betray Jesus.

Satan himself entered into Judas. I believe the threat
was too great and the end result too critical for Satan to
entrust this job to anyone else. He determined that he
personally would make sure that this man, Jesus, was
killed once and for all. Little did he know that by killing

Jesus, he would bring to spiritual life hundreds and thousands, eventually millions, of men and women just like Jesus.

Because Jesus came to the earth, was crucified, buried and raised from the dead, we can die to our old man [our old nature] and be raised again to newness of life through Jesus' sacrifice.

The Judas spirit is Satan. We must realize that Satan was able to enter Judas and use him for this evil even after Judas was so mightily used of God because *Judas was not born again.* The Spirit of God rested upon him but not *in him.*

Scripture tells us that an evil spirit and the Holy Spirit cannot be resident and in control of the same place at the same time. For example, the reborn spirit of man cannot be possessed of both the Holy Spirit and the devil. However, the devil can possess or control the mind (mental illness, confusion, oppression and depression) and the physical body (terminal or chronic illnesses) of a born-again believer, if that believer allows him entrance.

At the time the betrayal of Jesus took place, the devil only had to be concerned with one God man and a group of twelve, sometimes disorganized, possibly even confused, disciples. I'm sure Jesus was enough for Satan to be concerned about, but what I am saying is, at this time, everything threatening Satan's fragile kingdom took place in one small area of the world. The devil could be there to oversee it.

The problem Satan has now is that, unlike God, he is not omnipresent. He cannot be everywhere at once. There are now millions of followers of Jesus doing exactly as Jesus prophesied: **even greater works** (John 14:12).

The Judas spirit is the spirit of Satan. It is the spirit of Antichrist. Today if you, as a pastor, have a Judas spirit in your church, it's most likely *not* the devil himself but is, instead, a lower class of spirit or a demon. The only thing demons are good for is for running off. So how do you rid yourself of a Judas spirit? Cast him out and run him off in Jesus' name!

God has given us all authority over the powers and principalities of Satan, and in the name of Jesus, we *can* cast out demons.

You may be questioning, "But what about the people who are under his control?" If they want to be free, you can help them. If they don't, you must let them go before you, too, are betrayed.

It seems incomprehensible to me that Judas would allow himself to be used of the devil after seeing all that he had seen in Jesus' ministry.

> Jesus, knowing all that was going to happen to him, went out and asked them, "Who is it you want?"
>
> "Jesus of Nazareth," they replied. "I am he," Jesus said. (And Judas the traitor was standing there with them.)
>
> When Jesus said, "I am he," they drew back and fell to the ground.
>
> John 18:4-6

Even during the very last hours of Jesus' life on earth, Judas saw the power of God released when the words "I am He" were spoken by Jesus to the mob that came to take Him. Those three words and the power behind them caused the entire mob to fall backwards to the ground. It was at that very time that Jesus asked Judas if he would betray the Son of God with a kiss.

How could someone still continue to plot to betray Jesus after he had been identified by Jesus at the Last Supper as the one who would? It is impossible to understand! Demonic possession is the only answer. Judas was either unwilling or unable to change his mind.

Pray for wisdom as to how God would have you deal with individuals in Satan's bondage. Each person is worth saving, and God loves them all, but only those who *choose* to repent can and will be delivered.

9
The Judas Spirit Always Brings Death

While he was still speaking a crowd came up, and the man who was called Judas, one of the Twelve, was leading them. He approached Jesus to kiss him,

But Jesus asked him, "Judas, are you betraying the Son of Man with a kiss?"

Luke 22:47,48

The friendly gesture of a kiss started a process that would result in the death of the Son of God. Judas betrayed the Lord with a kiss. I can only assume that this is where we got the term, "The kiss of death."

Jesus made Himself accessible to arrest, but no one could take His life until He laid it down. Judas' betrayal brought about the death of Jesus, but what about Judas?

Early in the morning, all the chief priests and the elders of the people came to the decision to put Jesus to death.

They bound him, led him away and handed him over to Pilate, the governor.

When Judas, who had betrayed him, saw that Jesus was condemned, he was seized with remorse and returned the thirty silver coins to the chief priests and the elders.

"I have sinned," he said, "for I have betrayed innocent blood." "What is that to us?" they replied. "That's your responsibility."

So Judas threw the money into the temple and left.
Then he went away and hanged himself.

Matthew 27:1-5

As a result of Judas' actions, death came to Jesus. At the very moment Satan left Judas' body, Judas came to himself and realized, **I have sinned, for I have betrayed innocent blood.**

It is my desire that everyone who is being used by a Judas spirit would come to his senses and realize he is betraying innocent blood. "Innocent blood?" you might ask. "You don't know my pastor! He's always making mistakes. It seems he goes out of his way to offend me." The Word says, **Do not touch my anointed ones** (Psalm 105:15).

Until God sees fit to make you the pastor (and He never will if you are a betrayer), keep your mouth shut and pray for God to give you love and patience for your pastor. Trust me, that is probably what your pastor has asked God for — the love and patience to put up with you!

There is only One perfect Shepherd and that is Jesus Christ. There never has been and never will be a perfect sheep.

If you are being controlled by a Judas spirit, cast him off of you in Jesus' name. If you, as a pastor, are being harassed by a Judas spirit, God has given you the authority to cast out devils, so get rid of him.

If you have anyone on your staff or in your congregation who is being used by a Judas spirit, and they don't want to be delivered from it, tell them to leave. It takes more courage to remove a troublesome person than it takes to stand against him. The rest of the flock is too precious to be lost, hindered, or harassed because of one foolish sheep.

10

Love Will Overcome the Judas Spirit

If I speak in the tongues of men and of angels, but have not love, I am only a resounding gong or a clanging cymbal.

If I have the gift of prophecy and can fathom all mysteries and all knowledge, and I have a faith that can move mountains, but have not love, I am nothing.

If I give all I possess to the poor and surrender my body to the flames, but have not love, I gain nothing.

1 Corinthians 13:1-3

In an earlier chapter, I talked about my experiences at my home church. You may wonder whatever happened to the church and to the precious couple who endured such cruel abuse from a flock they so dearly loved.

I see the couple from time to time. They haven't pastored a church in several years. I believe the hurt was too deep and the rejection too painful for them to ever risk being hurt again. They did attempt to pastor other churches, but none were ever as successful as the ministry in my home church.

As for the town and the church, there have been over a dozen pastors in and out of that church. None have ever seen the fruit that was borne while the one couple pastored. How sad that because of a demonic, betrayal spirit, an entire generation, and possibly generations to come, will never know the saving grace of the Lord Jesus Christ. The cost is too great and time is too short to allow the Judas spirit to work in your church.

Satan delights in hindering a person's calling and in side-tracking God's purpose in their lives. Though the Judas spirit is a strong spirit, the good news is that the Judas spirit is not stronger than God's love, nor is it stronger than the God in you or me when we choose to love one another.

The couple who pastored tried to love these people and diligently taught them what Jesus said about loving one another. In fact, I remember the pastor would start teaching on a different subject, but the Spirit of God always brought him back to the subject of love.

One woman in the church became so enraged that at the end of one Sunday service, while threatening to slap the pastor, asked, "Why don't you ever teach about anything but love?"

The pastor, while prepared to duck, said, "If you will start to love, I'll stop teaching about love." The woman threw her hands up in rage and stomped out of the church mumbling as she went. What is amazing is that she was back for the next service as if nothing had happened. Her glares at the pastor, however, gave her away!

Because of the stress and pressure in the church, the pastor, even though he was a young man, had a massive heart attack. The assault of the betrayers became even more intense and evil. After the pastor's heart attack, they told all who would listen to them that it was God's punishment for the pastor's resistance to them.

While in the hospital, God performed a creative miracle. The doctor's diagnosis said up to 80 percent of his heart was damaged, he probably would never leave his bed, and if he did, he would definitely never work or pastor again.

God had a plan for this man's life. The pastor told me that late one night, while he was still in the hospital, he was awakened by footsteps coming down the hall. Thinking it was a nurse or doctor, he paid very little attention until the door opened.

In the light, he saw a man he didn't recognize come in and stand at the foot of his bed. The man called him by name and asked, "What do you want to do?" Suddenly, realizing that the man was Jesus, the pastor said, "Lord, I know You are not through with me. You have more for me to do."

Jesus touched and healed the pastor, and tests run the following day confirmed his healing. To the amazement of the doctors, the new tests showed that there was nothing wrong with his heart.

The betrayers, after hearing of his miraculous recovery, denied that it was God who healed him, and said it was the devil. Again, they told everyone who would listen, both saved and unsaved, that the pastor was surely demon-possessed for the devil to be able to do such a thing. Sounds like what the Pharisees said to Jesus when He healed a demon-possessed man.

"It is only by Beelzebub, the prince of demons, that this fellow drives out demons."

Jesus knew their thoughts and said to them, "Every kingdom divided against itself will be ruined, and every city or household divided against itself will not stand.

"If Satan drives out Satan, he is divided against himself. How then can his kingdom stand?

"And if I drive out demons by Beelzebub, by whom do your people drive them out? So then, they will be your judges.

"But if I drive out demons by the Spirit of God, then the kingdom of God has come upon you.

"Or again, how can anyone enter a strong man's house and carry off his possessions unless he first ties up the strong man? Then he can rob his house.

"He who is not with me is against me, and he who does not gather with me scatters.

"And so I tell you, every sin and blasphemy will be forgiven men, but the blasphemy against the Spirit will not be forgiven."

Matthew 12:24-31

This was a very sad part of my life, because some of my relatives, who had been saved and touched by this couple, were now bitter, confused and even afraid of them. This happened because a pastor reached out in love and challenged his church members to reach beyond the four walls of the church and do the same.

I don't believe any born-again believer sets out to be a betrayer and a blasphemer, but if we choose to stop loving, we will digress and become embittered and be a prime target to be used of the devil.

Love is patient, love is kind. It does not envy, it does not boast, it is not proud.

It is not rude, it is not self-seeking, it is not easily angered, it keeps no record of wrongs.

Love does not delight in evil but rejoices with the truth.

It always protects, always trusts, always hopes, always perseveres.

Love never fails....

1 Corinthians 13:4-8

Scripture is clear as to what love is and what it is not. When the Pharisees asked Jesus, **Which is the greatest commandment in the Law?** He answered:

"'Love the Lord your God with all your heart and with all your soul and with all your mind.'

"This is the first and greatest commandment.

"And the second is like it: 'Love your neighbor as yourself.'

"All the Law and the Prophets hang on these two commandments."

Matthew 22:37-40

What a powerful statement: **All the Law and the Prophets hang on these two commandments.** Everything God said and did hangs on our loving Him and loving one another.

I believe very few individuals, and even fewer church bodies, have reached this level of love, but it is obtainable or God wouldn't have challenged us to do it. Love, however, is not a feeling. It is a decision.

A Judas spirit cannot operate in an atmosphere of love.

And now these three remain: faith, hope and love. But the greatest of these is love.

1 Corinthians 13:13

11

After the Judas Spirit Is Defeated, What's Next?

Then they returned to Jerusalem from the hill called the Mount of Olives, a Sabbath day's walk from the city.

When they arrived, they went upstairs to the room where they were staying. Those present were Peter, John, James and Andrew; Philip and Thomas, Bartholomew and Matthew; James son of Alphaeus and Simon the Zealot, and Judas the son of James.

They all joined together constantly in prayer, along with the women and Mary the mother of Jesus, and with his brothers.

In those days Peter stood up among the believers (a group numbering about a hundred and twenty)

And said, "Brothers, the Scripture had to be fulfilled which the Holy Spirit spoke long ago through the mouth of David concerning Judas, who served as guide for those who arrested Jesus —

"He was one of our number and shared in this ministry."

(With the reward he got for his wickedness, Judas bought a field; there he fell headlong, his body burst open and all his intestines spilled out.

Everyone in Jerusalem heard about this, so they called that field in their language Akeldama, that is, Field of Blood.)

"For," said Peter, "it is written in the book of

Psalms, `May his place be deserted; let there be no one to dwell in it,' and `May another take his place of leadership.'

"Therefore, it is necessary to choose one of the men who have been with us the whole time the Lord Jesus went in and out among us,

"Beginning from John's baptism to the time when Jesus was taken up from us. For one of these must become a witness with us of his resurrection."

Acts 1:12-22

Once the person who has been controlled by the Judas spirit repents and is delivered, then healing can take place and unity can be restored. If the person is not repentive and refuses to be delivered, he (or she) should be removed. Replace the person with someone you know, for scripture admonishes that we **know those who labor among us** (1 Thessalonians 5:12).

Unity Brings Power

Acts 2:1-4 says:

When the day of Pentecost came, they were all together in one place.

Suddenly a sound like the blowing of a violent wind came from heaven and filled the whole house where they were sitting.

They saw what seemed to be tongues of fire that separated and came to rest on each of them.

All of them were filled with the Holy Spirit and began to speak in other tongues as the Spirit enabled them.

As pastors, ministers and lay members, unity should be a primary goal in our churches. To see the present-day Church joined together in one accord like the First Century Church is God's heart's desire, and if it is that important to God, it should be equally important to His Body.

If you, as a pastor, will deal with the Judas spirit and remove it from the church, unity will come and the power of God will manifest in your midst.

Summary

The Spirit of the Lord is on me, because he has anointed me to preach the good news to the poor. He has sent me to proclaim freedom for the prisoners and recovery of sight to the blind, to release the oppressed,

To proclaim the year of the Lord's favor.

Luke 4:18,19

My purpose for writing this book is not to set people straight, but it is to set them *FREE*. My concern is for anyone who has dealt with, or ever will deal with, people controlled by a betraying spirit.

The main part of this book is informational, although the subject is an emotional one. I would be lax in my obedience to God if I did not share with you my emotions, both now and when some of these events took place.

The call to ministry in my life came when I was twelve years of age. It was a strong, definite call, but I had no one to counsel, encourage, or guide me. There was no one to ask, "What's next?" so I didn't respond to the call until much later in life. Part of the reason for the length of time for my response to God's call had to do with the anger and despair I felt from the hurts of the church split and the fighting among the brethren.

I was saved in this church at the age of seven and sat under the pastor's guidance and teaching for eleven years. They were my family, friends and examples of what being a Christian was supposedly all about.

With the fighting and the eventual split of the church, my feelings of security and belonging crashed. Confusion, anger and hopelessness overwhelmed me.

I attended Bible college in another city, owned and operated by the same church denomination I had attended. Because my family and I stood up in support of the pastors, I was somewhat blacklisted at first but was more accepted later. Even though I did well in college, there was an angry fire inside me that needed to be dealt with.

After college, I tried to help in churches with the youth and children, but I became more depressed and angry as time went on. Eventually, I rejected the church and all it stood for and began to look for love and acceptance in the world. Rebellion, drugs, sex and everything else I tried could not fill the void in my life.

Ten years later, after a broken marriage and a long list of people I had let down and hurt, I found what I was looking for —a church family that was loving and unified. I wanted so desperately to know God was on my side, not because of being right or wrong in the things that had happened, or in our support of the pastor couple; I simply had to know that God loved me and wanted the best for me.

I had heard people say that God was on their side, yet saw them do horrible things to others. I needed to know the love of God was real and available to someone like me.

As I shared with you the experiences in the church of my childhood, you may be asking, "What were the members of the church who were supporters of the pastors doing while these atrocities took place?"

For the most part, we watched in dismay, simply because we didn't understand or know what else we were to do. That's not to say that we didn't speak up and say it was wrong. However, when we did say something in defense of the pastors, we were reminded by the church leaders that we were not on the same spiritual plain as they were and we could not possibly understand what was taking place.

Praise God! No one can ever say that to you, for you now know what to look for and you are not ignorant of the devil's devices. The purposes of God are not to be a mystery to you or me. He wants us to know what is true and what is false. Romans 3:4 says, **Let God be true, and every man a liar.**

My desire is that no one will ever experience what I did, nor be guilty of being used as a betrayer.

There is not enough time or print for me to tell you all the people who were hurt and are still hurting from what took place in one little church.

The fleshly failings of one person, minister, or pastor cannot cause me to fall or turn back. I couldn't have said that a few years ago, but I can say it now because *my hope is built on nothing less than Jesus Christ and His righteousness!*

My prayer is that your hope is built on Jesus Christ and not on man. May God bless you as you live and move and have your being in Him, knowing who the enemy is and how to defeat him!